HAIKU

俳句

HAIKU

POETRY ANCIENT & MODERN

an anthology
compiled by

JACKIE HARDY

TUTTLE PUBLISHING
Tokyo • Rutland, Vermont • Singapore

First published in the United States in
2002 by Tuttle Publishing, an imprint
of Periplus Editions (HK) Ltd., with
editorial offices at 364 Innovation Drive,
North Clarendon, Vermont 05759

Copyright © Octopus Publishing Group
Ltd

Designer: Bet Ayer
Editor: Kate John
Library of Congress Catalog Card
Number. 2001099494

ISBN: 978-0-8048-3858-0

Distributed by

**North America, Latin America
& Europe**
Tuttle Publishing
364 Innovation Drive
North Clarendon, VT 05759-9436
Tel: (802) 773-8930
Fax: (802) 773-6993
info@tuttlepublishing.com
www.tuttlepublishing.com

Asia Pacific
Berkeley Books Pte. Ltd.
61 Tai Seng Avenue #02-12
Singapore 534167
Tel: (65) 6280-1330
Fax: (65) 6280-6290
inquiries@periplus.com.sg
www.periplus.com

Japan
Tuttle Publishing
Yaekari Building, 3rd Floor
5-4-12 Osaki
Shinagawa-ku
Toky 141 0032
Tel: (03) 5437-0171
Fax: (03) 5437-0755
tuttle-sales@gol.com

First edition
09 08 07   9 8 7 6 5 4 3
Printed in China

# contents

introduction

do you remember, as a small child, when all words were a delight? Can you recall the thrill of hearing a new word, one that you wanted to say over and over? Perhaps it rhymed with one which you already knew, and you connected them again and again into your own poem. A poem that played and played in your head. Perhaps, for a while, it became your mantra, protecting you and befriending you. Then just as suddenly it was ousted by another word, replaced with another poem with which you became spellbound. Can you recall that magical time when words took on significance beyond their meaning?

For me, haiku provide a grown-up version of this magic. With their infinite variety of subjects and images, haiku offer opportunities to experience things you could not otherwise "know." For the writer, haiku not only express a moment of insight, but a reconnection with that time when words were a talisman. For me, there is no wonder, then, that the haiku form is practiced around the globe. In their unique, small way, haiku show what it is to be human.

Haiku originated in seventeenth century Japan. One of its poetic antecedents is to be found in *renga*, a form of collaborative poem where three, four or more enthusiasts would got together to compose elegant verses. This major form of Japanese poetry flourished in the fourteenth and fifteenth centuries and was written to strict rules. As befits its importance, the opening verse or *hokku*, was written most often by the honored guest in a three phase, seventeen syllable form arranged in a 5-7-5 pattern. The entertainment would continue as poets took turns to compose links, until there was a poetic sequence of usually one hundred verses. Over the years the hokku began to stand alone and become independent of the rest of the sequence.

As literacy increased in the sixteenth century, so did the popularity of this type of pastime. All classes of people became involved in composing a particularly light-hearted form of renga, called *haikai*. Haikai, with its more relaxed attitude to good taste, was characterized by witticism, puns, slang terms, its subject matter no longer elevated, often vulgar. Many poets found it more enjoyable to abandon the idea of linking verses, and they began to compose only the hokku. It was the poet Shiki (1867–1902) who advocated distinguishing between the independent verse and that of the opening verse of a renga sequence. The former he designated haiku.

It takes a singular culture in which the composition of poetry becomes a popular pastime. What, then, were the factors significant in highlighting the poetical nature of the Japanese character?

As well as renga, Chinese poetry and *waka* or *tanka*, a short poem also using 5-7-5 syllable constructions, influenced the writing of haiku. Chinese poetry had been familiar to the upper classes and dwellers in the Japanese court for centuries and the practice of writing love poetry and verses for the significant occasion, as well as the ordinary, was commonplace. But haiku has always been more than a literary convention. A notable part of the form embraced by the serious practitioner was the spiritual aspect.

Japan has been subject to a forest of invading spiritual ideas, philosophies and religions. A tall tree of this forest is Buddhism, seeds of which came from India via China and then branched out into Zen, the characteristics of which most attracted those of the Japanese. Many of the early renga masters were monks. The most famous of all was Basho (1644–94) whose haiku followers were also prepared to be disciples because of his deep interest in Zen.

Taoism, Confucianism and Shinto, the religion native to Japan, have also deeply affected the Eastern creative mind.

What then, with all these influences might we expect to find in the composition of a Japanese haiku? Buddhism has donated a simple directness and instantaneous perception. Zen, a paradoxical convergence of the practical and the ideal. Taoism has contributed allegory and the philosophy of the "way," where writing haiku becomes a mindset, a way of living. Confucianism gave substance, brevity, reserve. Shinto; mythology and animatism.

Different schools of haiku writing developed in Japan: One school, which followed the traditional, more formal conventions; and one which led a radical approach. Each group had its enthusiasts. Haiku has experienced periods of change and reconstruction, but its appeal remains. Today, in Japan, it is said, there are over eight hundred groups writing and sharing haiku.

Haiku's arrival in the West early in the twentieth century has been well documented. It influenced the Imagists, the Beat poets and those who began to read translations of Chinese and Japanese classics by R. H. Blyth. Some readers and writers began to look for similarities of form, spirit, or theme in English poets and have made cases for such similarities in Wordsworth, Shelley and Keats. Others conned the work of more obscure writers such as John Clare, Gilbert White, and Richard Jeffries and found similarities, which were worth the comparison. Until the 1990s the practice of writing haiku in the West remained the way of a few. Sometime in the early nineties, however, haiku experienced that coming-together-of-all-the-right-factors-event and, instead of a limbering-up exercise for those wanting to write "real" poetry, it became widely recognized as a literary form, a discipline in its own right, known of and practiced by many more people. Societies devoted to the enjoyment and dissemination of haiku were founded in countries across the world, it was taught and assessed in schools, and some mainstream poets included the form in their published collections.

It can be seen, then, that compared to the long, distinguished history of the haiku form in Asia, it is early days for Western haiku. In Japan the form is brief, usually connected to the season in which it is written, in the present tense and often containing 17 syllables in the 5-7-5 pattern. Haiku's connection with nature is profound, and as nature and human nature are intertwined in Japanese thought, one may be used to highlight insights about the other.

In spite of its infancy in the West, haiku has features of its own, a distinctive voice and a predisposition to change and develop. In the English speaking world it is less common for haiku to be written in the 17 syllable, 5-7-5 pattern. The structure of the Japanese language lends itself to that pattern naturally, rhythmically, and historically. Some Western haiku poets enjoy the challenge

of the syllable count and the first example in this anthology, by Brian Cater, testifies to its possibilities;

> this long recession:
> at the end of my tee–square
> a spider starts work

Other haiku writers see the 17 syllable pattern as an irrelevant phenomenon when writing in English. The varying length of the English language syllable, as against that of the consistent length of the Japanese *onji*, and English's ability to convey meaning in a more economical way, usually result in haiku of fewer syllables, sometimes much fewer, as in this example by Giovanni Malito;

> low tide
> the driftwood
> rests

The 5-7-5 pattern has also been responsible for most Western haiku appearing in a three-line form. Most of the poems in this anthology conform to this convention, but it is not rare to see haiku taking other shapes. This anthology gives examples of a two-liner from David Cobb;

> **across the fields of stubble**
> **flame   stalks   flame**

and Alexis Rotella's four-liner;

> **among morning glories**
> **the drip**
> **drip**
> **   of lingerie**

Lee Guiseck's haiku—

> **dry well**
> **the dropped stone's**
> **   thud**

is an example of both the very short haiku and a four-liner. The empty third line pushes this haiku towards the concrete form. Clearly, these are the most appropriate shapes for what they are trying to convey.

Some Western poets have abandoned the seasonal reference in an attempt to broaden haiku themes from the natural and to include technology or modern ideas. In the above examples there is seasonal imagery or a reference to the natural world of plants, insects, weather or indeed atmosphere, explicit in all of them. Apart from Lee Guiseck's haiku's more complex form, each of these haiku employ the present tense of the verb, giving it immediacy and highlighting that moment of insight which inspired the poet. The present tense aids the poets' involvement in the things surrounding that moment of inspiration, enhancing feelings and perceptions that could be lost in the craft of creation. Many haiku, however, work well by using the present participle of the verb and there are many examples of such in this anthology.

Any poetical form conforms to some conventions. With haiku it is often easier to talk in negative terms, for example no title, punctuation or capital letters. The brevity of the form encourages a precise and plain language, direct and objective, where each word must work hard to maintain its place. Haiku have been described as the poem of a single breath. This short span highlights the transience of the evocation of experience, the transience of life. Haiku are open-ended, pointing out the mystery and depth of emotional experience, the ambiguity of the joyfulness and the futility of any moment. The haiku poet makes no attempt to intellectualize the experience and in some senses haiku are a creative offering straight from the heart. However, conventions are there to be flouted: Development and dynamism need change.

For the purposes of selecting haiku for this anthology I have chosen to use the themes of the five elements in Taoist cosmology—wood, fire, earth, metal and water. These elements are dynamic, driven by the underlying

nature of yin and yang, which as opposites, need to interact if there is to be spark, dynamism, and energy in the universe. Yin and yang are complementary yet antagonistic forces, which have the following properties: Yang is associated with Heaven, and is harder, hotter, brighter, more active; yin is associated with the Earth, and is softer, cooler, darker, passive.

The energy created by the interaction of yin and yang is cyclical; each five-element cycle supports the next. This is most often seen in two cycles, one productive or nourishing, where the rising energy of wood is the creator of fire, while fire in turn nourishes and forms soil, compost or earth. Given time and pressure, the earth, which contains ore, is the creator of the element metal.

Under the duress of the yang influence, metal will metaphorically melt or liquify, and this stage is known as water. In turn water supports and nourishes plant life, creating the element wood. The other cycle is the destructive or controlling cycle, where water impedes the effect of fire, which reduces the quality of metal, which restrains wood, which reduces earth, which goes on to complete the cycle by blocking water.

The five elements have a number of qualities. I have applied such qualities to the main subject or image or seasonal reference in the chosen haiku, and they have been allotted to a heading accordingly.

Wood embodies the spirit of initiation and dawn. The element that brings freshness to the cycle, wood represents spring, youth, vitality, energy, inspiration and enthusiasm. It is associated with the color green and the direction east.

Fire is represented by the feverish activity of midsummer or midday. Red is fire's color and its direction, south.

Earth represents the energy of the afternoon, the late summer and is a mellow, quiet period. The color associated with it is yellow. Earth is the center. The theme of Indian summer connects disparate images in this section.

Metal represents the energy of the evening. Seasonally, it is autumn, the traditional time for gathering and storing and completing tasks. The direction is west and its associated color is white.

Water embodies the floating, restful time that is winter or the night. Water's color is black. This peaceful, restful time is regenerative, and restorative, and the associated direction is north.

Finally, within the constriction of my selected themes, I have chosen what I liked. There is a mixture of classical and modern haiku. Where the haiku are translated I have chosen my favorite one from among several. I have endeavored to show why haiku's appeal is universal and lasting, and the scope and depth of its representation of human experience.

JACKIE HARDY

wood

this long recession:
at the end of my tee-square
    a spider starts work

BRIAN CATER

morning sneeze
the guitar in the corner
resonates

DEE EVETTS

where knights lived—
wormholes in the timbers
shedding no more dust

DAVID COBB

dusk fades to peach—
wasps tenderly brushing against
splintered barn wood

WALLY SWIST

sculptor's studio
   from the drying wood
a tiny spider

KAREN KLEIN

planing old roof joists
and in the wood grain finding
winter landscapes

DAVID PLATT

plank bridge—
clinging for their lives
ivy vines

BASHO

housecleaning day—
hanging a shelf at his home
a carpenter

BASHO

thunder
my woodshavings roll
along the veranda

DEE EVETTS

wooden gate,
lock firmly bolted:
winter moon

KIKAKU

old garden shed
the insecticide can
full of spiders

ERNEST BERRY

without a thought
the neighbor's back yard
turns green

WILLIAM J HIGGINSON

storm—chestnuts
race along
the bamboo porch
SHIKI

from which tree's blossom
it comes, I do not know
this fragrance

BASHO

the beechwood hedge
taking shape
with each clip
a puff of flies

NORMAN BARRACLOUGH

bad-tempered, I got back
then, in the garden
the willow tree

RYOTA

my temporary shelter—
a pasania tree is here, too
in this summer grove

BASHO

smoothing paper
on my fingertips
the roughness of words

JACKIE HARDY

beautiful, seen through holes
made in the paper screen:
the Milky Way

ISSA

this year
through the dying cherry
so much more sky

SUSAN ROWLEY

willow and cherry
willow and cherry—
riverbank

KODOJIN

full moon
over my father's orchard—
the thump of an apple

RICH KRIVCHER

as raindrops diminish
I hear the tapping
of the monk's wooden bell

PATRICIA DONEGAN

watching the ducks
season after season
a wooden heron

MICHAEL GUNTON

quietening the mind
deep in the forest
water drips

HOSHA

spring thaw:
the old pine leans a little
farther this year

VIRGINIA EGERMEIER

weathered wooden walk
grains of sand blown in, blown out
of a knothole

CHRISTOPHER HEROLD

the coolness—
growing straight, the branches
of a wild pine

BASHO

the pines careen
the way the rough waves
crash

SANTOKA

on a pine trunk
the tall black shadow
of another pine

JACKIE HARDY

village has grown old—
not a single house without
persimmon trees

BASHO

an aging willow
   its image unsteady
      in the flowing stream

ROBERT SPIESS

harvest moon:
on the bamboo mat
pine-tree shadows

KIKAKU

sweet chestnut in flower
a curved bough holding
the evening sun

CICELY HILL

the ancient pollard
its dead bole mingled
with leaf shadow

NORMAN BARRACLOUGH

above the noise
of the motorway
wind in the poplars

MARTIN LUCAS

on a bare branch
a crow has alighted...
autumn nightfall

BASHO

in the bush
the scent of wild orchids
from a rotting tree

ELENA LINDSEY

winter morning
without leaf or flower
the shape of the tree

L A DAVIDSON

slowly,
over cedars
sunshine, showers

GYODAI

their laughter…
the woods filled with white trillium
and sunshine

BETTY DREVNIOK

felling a tree
and gazing at the cut end—
tonight's moon

BASHO

along the way
an old oak branch
becomes a walking stick

GARRY GAY

anguish deepened
by the woodpecker's
distant hammering

JANICE BOSTOK

October maples—
through so many colours
so much light

KATHLEEN BASFORD

crow's abandoned nest
a plum tree

BASHO

rushing across the rocks
the felled tree's shadow

SUE STANFORD

brushwood bones
pruned and lopped,
yet budding branches

BONCHO

dusk
ravens
exchange trees

NOOR SINGH KHALSA

winter morning stillness
chopping wood
between the echoes

BYRON JACKSON

where the end
of a pine branch curves,
a squirrel's tail

KEITH COLEMAN

casting off the lines
    odour from the wooden wharf
   of drying dew

ROBERT SPIESS

toward the brushwood gate
it sweeps the tea leaves
stormy wind

BASHO

spring darkness:
in a world that drips & trickles
scent of the conifer grove

KEITH COLEMAN

winter maple
stripped of everything
but a blue kite

WINONA BAKER

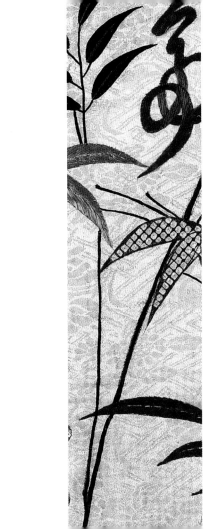

stacking firewood
scent
of the old forest

RUTH DALLAS

flickering
in the woodpile
the groundhog's eyes

JOE NUTT

piled for burning
brushwood
starts to bud

BONCHO

slipping downhill
the darkness
of trees

PENNY HARTER

locked in for the winter...
again I'll be nestling close
to this post

BASHO

stacking wood—
maple trees
the colour of fire

ANN GOLDRING

long after
the leaping buck—the quiver
of the fencepost

GEORGE SWEDE

fire

across the fields of stubble
flame   stalks   flame

DAVID COBB

flaring match
just a glimpse
of wrinkled faces

GRAHAM DUNN

thumbprint left
in the candle wax—
August heat

JIM KACIAN

brushing away the ashes
a single smoked sardine

BONCHO

a fool in the dark
        grabs a bramble—
        firefly hunt

the autumn mountains
here and there
smoke rising

GYODAI

campfire—
shadows of the men disappear
into the woods

JIM KACIAN

lighting the fire
those first flames
catching last year's news

JACKIE HARDY

campfire extinguished
the woman washing dishes
in a pan of stars

RAYMOND ROSELIEP

dozing on horseback
smoke from the tea-fires
drifts to the moon

BASHO

the cooing of a turtle dove
in the sound of
a bonfire

CHICHIBA MESAKU

log fire
turning in the flames
my watched thoughts

CAROLINE GOURLAY

old electric fire
discarded in the garden
heated by spring sun

COLIN BLUNDELL

our old charcoal grill,
still cradling last year's cold ash
a sudden shiver

ALAN MALEY

midnight heat
fireflies travel
in the river's echo

HUMBERTO GATICA

around the campfire
singing every song we know
to keep warm

KATHERINE GALLAGHER

by firelight
listening to the silence
of things we can't see

LARRY GROSS

this charcoal fire—
our years fall away
in just that fashion

SHIKI

firefly viewing
her feet...
        feeling for the path

CYRIL CHILDS

midnight sun—
spider's silhouette floats
between two pines

JASON MURRAY

turning the pillow—
even under there
the heat of tonight

GEOFFREY DANIEL

embers die
the chair where the friend sat
fills with moonlight

CICELY HILL

thirteenth century glass
catches fire
late afternoon

high above the city
dawn flares
from a window-washer's pail

COR VAN DEN HEUVEL

in the leaky boat
blowfly on the lamplighter—
star beyond the sea

CLELIA IFRIM

waiting for fireworks—
old stone warehouse stares
from across the flume

H F NOYES

the lantern blown out—
the sound of the wind
through the leaves

SHIKI

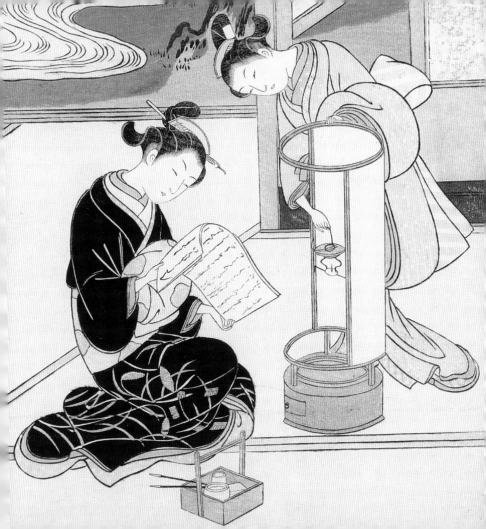

lantern on an old road
it gathers round
so much night

NICHOLAE IONEL

stirring the embers
our conversation
silent for a moment

HARSANGEET KAUR BHULLAR

summer lightning
yesterday in the east
today in the west

KIKAKU

falling leaves
the chess game ends
by lamplight

DORIS HEITMEYER

glancing behind
they are lighting the barrier lanterns
in the evening haze

TAIGI

on the edge of the veranda
even so few fireworks
gives the feeling of night

ISSA

firefly viewing,...
and just as one stumbles—
look, there's a firefly

ISSA

lighting the candles
in the thatched temple
plum blossoms fall

GYODAI

in the corpse's
half-closed eyes
the flame of a candle

VASILE SPINEI

a white petal falls
in the heavy air—
summer lightning

CLAIRE BUGLER HEWITT

candlelight dinner—
his finger slowly circles
the rim of his glass

LEE GURGA

stillness—
the candle flame
grows

GEORGE MARSH

clouds like
thrown fire
—magnolia flowers

ASUKA NOMIYAMA

A flash of lightning
where there were faces
plumes of pampas grass

BASHO

lighting the lantern
the yellow of chrysanthemums
fades

BUSON

thundery air
infused with insects
tea on the lawn

CAROLINE GOURLAY

heat lightning—
fireflies across the meadow
without a sound

JIM KACIAN

red geraniums
  rips in the awning
  leak sunlight

ELLEN COMPTON

red light
sloshing of the gasoline
in the tank

ANDRE DUHAIME

I look at my scar
remembering the dark crimson
of autumn roses

ROSY WILSON

loneliness
after the fireworks
a falling star

SHIKI

burning old letters—
a page leaps out
to scorch the mat

ELENA LINDSEY

summer grasses
all that remains
of soldiers' dreams

BASHO

watering the beans
   in the cool of the evening
     a fiery sun

JIM NORTON

earth

土

freshly spaded plot
   a flock of sparrows
   taking dust baths

PHYLLIS WALSH

when the spade turns
the earth in our garden—
how different it is

ION CODRESCU

day's end
emptying the beach
from my shoe

PAMELA MILLER NESS

in the morning dew
spotted with mud, and how cool—
melons on the soil

BASHO

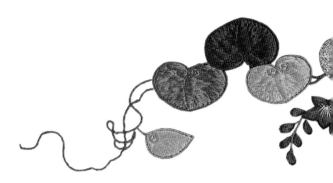

morris dancers
tread old patterns
into summer turf

SUSAN ROWLEY

downpour—
a pinnacle of soil topped
with a tiny stone

SUE STANFORD

only the stone-smell
tells of it…
summer rain

KENNETH TANEMURA

dry well
the dropped stone's

thud

LEE GIESECKE

the cold night
comes out of the stones
all morning

JIM KACIAN

in the icy moonlight
small stones
crunch underfoot

BUSON

in the garden
the silence of stones
under snow

ERIC L HOUCH JR

first snow
    the neglected yard
    now perfect

ELIZABETH ST JACQUES

spring planting
from eyes of one potato
a dozen plants

L A DAVIDSON

travelling through the world—
to and fro, to and fro
harrowing the small field

BASHO

rows of corn
stretch to the horizon—
sun on the thunderhead

LEE GURGA

in the corner of the field
bunching up and singing—
frogs

KODOJIN

indian summer:
    the scarecrow's jacket fades
        to a paler blue

LORRAINE ELLIS HAAR

after the quake
the weathervane
pointing to earth

MICHAEL DYLAN WELCH

flag-covered coffin
the shadow of the bugler
slips into the grave

NICHOLAS VIRGILIO

the earth shakes
just enough
to remind us

STEVE SANFIELD

turning from her grave
the tug of a rose thorn
on my padded sleeve

DAVID COBB

only the staffs
  of the pilgrims are seen going
  through the summer fields

BASHO

tilling the field
the cloud that never moved
has gone

BUSON

ill on a journey
over parched fields
dreams wander on

BASHO

quiet country road
dusty sweetness
of ripe raspberries

JEAN JORGENSEN

waft your fragrance
on a hill where they mine coal
plum blossoms

BASHO

on this mountain
      sorrow...tell me about it
  digger of wild yams

indian summer:
dragonfly shadows seldom
brush the window

SHIKI

wind in the sagebush
the same dusty color
the smell of it

ELIZABETH S LAMB

daylight fading
a curlew's cry
lengthens the hill

CAROLINE GOURLAY

climbing down
feeling the avalanche
in each stone

TOM WILLIAMSON

statues in the square:
the raised hand of the war hero
fills with snow

GEORGE SWEDE

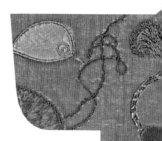

neolithic temple
under the massive stone
a column of ants

JACKIE HARDY

we leave
and the stone parrot glows
in the evening sun

BAN'YA NATSUSHI

in the chapel
caught by the autumn sunlight
a stone rose

MICHAEL GUNTON

a cold blast,
small stones rattle
across the planks of the roof

BUSON

the stillness!
the voice of the cicadas
sinks into the rocks

BASHO

at the window:
the earth drawn inwards
this still night

CICELY HILL

darkening road
wind parts the fur
of the dead cat

DEE EVETTS

the harvest moon—
I stroll round the pond
till the night is through

BASHO

during the sermon
I clean the week
from my nails

LEROY GORMAN

after the holiday
sand...
in my pocket

CYRIL CHILDS

butterflies flit...
that is all, amid the field
of sunlight

along the mountain road
somehow it tugs at my heart
a wild violet

BASHO

metal

leaden sky
the big wheel
still

MARTIN LUCAS

the blind musician
extending an old tin cup
collects a snowflake

NICHOLAS VIRGILIO

next to the battleship
a small boat
casting for mullet

KODOJIN

on a rusty buoy
the fog bell feels
each melancholy wave

GEORGE MARSH

166

town dump:
jabbering on a old brass bed
two magpies

GEORGE SWEDE

rusted train tracks...
a young maple
turning red

BETTY DREVNIOK

soon to die,
yet noisier than ever
the autumn cicada

SHIKI

travelling
old armour,
a glistening slug

RANSETSU

after a journey
the kettle—
ticking as it cools

JIM NORTON

summer's end
the quickening of hammers
 towards dusk

DEE EVETTS

school bell rings
 all of the shadows
  into one

RUBY SPRIGGS

chill night
first knocks
from the radiator

MAURICE TASNIER

wedding ring worn thin
she kneads dough
in autumn sunlight

JOHN O'CONNOR

loose now
on her knuckle
the thin gold

SUSAN ROWLEY

framing the space
where she once was—
my mother's ring

DON MCLEOD

before the ferry
leaving a beggar
with all our change

MATT MORDEN

in his box
four or five coppers,
and now
the evening drizzle

evening bell:
persimmons pelt
the temple garden

SHIKI

iron autumn
and all the cold
windbells tinkling

DAKOTSU

feeling lonely
he strikes the gong again,
guard of the hill-paddy

SEKITEI

beneath
 the morning glory
 rusted steel

ERIC L HOUCH JR

swans gliding by—
the fastidious docking
of a rusty tug

DAVID COBB

the bitter morning—
a sudden shudder jolts through
a row of freight cars…

JERRY BALL

a note from the bell—
a cry from the water fowl—
and the night darkens

ISSA

empty silo
spring wind pops the metal
in and out

MICHAEL DYLAN WELCH

undressed:
today's role dangles
from a metal hanger

ALEXIS ROTELLA

streaming tufts of fleece
caught up on the barbed wire fence
the wind in our hair

NORMAN BARRACLOUGH

thin wire
the paper angel
vibrates

RAFFAEL DE GRUTTOLA

cool morning ground mist
the gate handle down
to bare metal

GARY HOTHAM

autumn comes
rust deepens
on the unused tracks

LAWRENCE RUNGREN

winter solstice:
the darkness closes in
against the church bells

KATHERINE GALLAGHER

rusty toy truck
stuck on the mudbank—
a cargo of blossoms

H F NOYES

Contending—
temple bell,
winter wind

KITO

behind locked steel gates
a shrieking game of tag
in the synagogue yard

WILLIAM HART

shrouding the old car
red virginia creeper
and rust

FERRIS GILLI

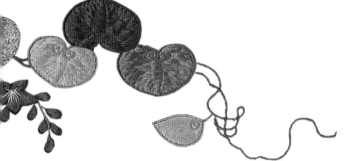

gentle as a dead friend's hand
resting on my shoulder
this autumn sunshine

KUSADAO

at the quick-serve till
checked out with each item
her engagement ring

DAVID COBB

this evening stillness…
just the rusted cowbell
found by the pasture gate

FOSTER JEWELL

autumn drizzle
the rusted tricycle
in the river bed

GARRY GAY

dying vibrations
on the TV aerial—
pigeon on the wing

NORMAN BARRACLOUGH

sewing cobwebs
in its corner—
the old Singer

LEO LAVERY

on the axe-head
the smell
split
out of kindling

GEOFFREY DANIEL

tea-kettle
hooked mid-air
towards heaven

HAKUIN

shingle beach
        rusty iron &
    seaweed tangle

M A R T I N   L U C A S

hailstones
into my iron bowl for alms

SANTOKA

heedless that the bell
tolls our time away,
we take the evening cool

ISSA

cold hands
deep in my pocket
forgotten coin

JACKIE HARDY

tolling bell
forget-me-nots
spill rain

SUEZAN AIKINS

no change—
I toss a leaf into
the public fountain

ROBERT EPSTEIN

on the barbed wire fence
sheep's wool plaited
by the wind

DAVID ROLLINS

old bike mender
hammering echoes
across the creek

JACKIE HARDY

reflected
in the sword's blade
soft summer clouds

GARRY GAY

overnight
my razor rusted—
the May rains

BONCHO

invading the quay
where the battleships
used to berth
red valerian

JOHN SHIMMIN

water

水

shipping oars
I hold my breath to hear
snow on the water

DAVID STEELE

on the rock
waves don't reach
fresh snow

TANTAN

the turtle's plash
just around the bend
a river Baptism

VINCENT TRIPI

overflowing the bucket
at the side of the well—
bush clover

KODOJIN

today's lunch:
only water

SANTOKA

spring rain:
in our sedan
your soft whispers

BUSON

from the bough
floating down the river
insect song

ISSA

one word
but so many varieties
of rain

DAVID FINLAY

deep bend in the brook
        the kingfisher's chatter
after its dive

WALLY SWIST

girls planting paddy:
only their song
free of mud

RAIZAN

the whole yard quiet—
the cool sound of rain
on rhubarb leaves

H F NOYES

shooting the rapids
even the back of his head
looks surprised

H F N O Y E S

little boy
discovers the world—
puddle after puddle

BERTUS DE JONGE

where sea and sky meet
only hazy fishing boats
dividing the gray

L A DAVIDSON

ebb tide
 every footprint leaves
another moon

MARIKAY ELDRIDGE

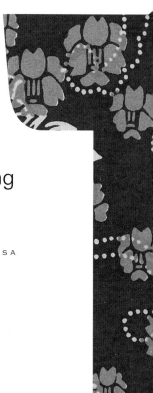

nightingale's song
this morning
soaked with rain

ISSA

short cut;
splashing through the water
of summer rains

BUSON

clear cascades—
into the waves scatter
green pine needles

BASHO

April shower—
my girlfriend's house key
back on my key ring

MICHAEL DYLAN WELCH

this rainy night
out wandering anywhere
the wet leaves point

MARIANNE BLUGER

in the well bucket
a morning glory
allows me some water

CHIYO-JO

the old pond:
a frog jumps in
   the sound of water

BASHO

long seasonal rain—
looking for the floating nest
of a grebe

BASHO

new kite—
the impatient child
in unending rain

SHOHA

even in the spring mists
the sounds of water
trickling through the
rocks

SOKAN

on our backs
a shower blown
from the waterfall

M A T T   M O R D E N

the May rains
even a nameless stream
is a thing of dread

BUSON

all night long
the sound of the waterfall
a remembered dream

JACKIE HARDY

petals of the mountain rose
fall now and then
to the roar of the waterfall

BASHO

even this tiny stone
is also wet
with dew

KYOSHI

winter solstice
  the waterfall frozen
in mid-air

SANDRA FUHRINGER

a light rain
into the evening mist
woodsmoke

BRIAN TASKER

a splash somewhere—
dark ripples
reach my toes

ARWYN EVANS

a long meeting
ice cubes in the jug
the first to leave

MATT MORDEN

overflowing the bucket
at the side of the well—
bush clover

KODOJIN

watering the yard
the sun-warm nozzle
turns chill in my hand

PAUL O WILLIAMS

among morning glories
the drip
    drip
        of lingerie

ALEXIS ROTELLA

hot bath water
cold on the breastless side
spring thunder

YOKO OGINO

winter rain—
people have been so kind
my eyes fill with tears

SANTOKA

river nighwinds—
a woman dips her wash
in the rippling moon

H F NOYES

summer twilight
a woman's song
mingles with the bath water

PATRICIA DONEGAN

240

spring rain—
down along a wasp's nest, water
leaking through the roof

BASHO

lake's brown surface
suddenly glinting
scarlet, orange...the koi

BERNARD GADD

third year of drought
lakes slow retreat
into itself

JEAN JORGENSEN

after the flood
  the album with old photos
  lies under the fence

VASILE SPINEI

fields flooded
beneath the surface, somewhere
the river bends

CHRISTOPHER HEROLD

flooded meadow—
crickets cling to the riggings
in the grass clumps

H F NOYES

empty playground
under every swing
a hollow of rain

TOM TICO

a bitter rain—
two silences
beneath
the one umbrella

GEOFFREY DANIEL

on the porch
   galoshes
full of rain

GEORGE SWEDE

stirring the last light
of day into the lake
the webbed feet of geese

JEFF WITKIN

darkness,
   wet with
the sound of waves

SANTOKA

between the rocks
water the ocean
didn't take back

GARY HOTHAM

low tide
the driftwood
rests

GIOVANNI MALITO

wild sea...
reaching across to Sado
the Milky Way

BASHO

waves crash
against the fortifications
dead of night

MICHAEL GUNTON

haiku authors

picture credits